bleach

by Steven W. Simon

Books by Steven W. Simon

Novels & Novellas
Ava in Lost Pines
1200 Miles from Los Angeles
Into the Fracking Fields
Red as Apple

Poetry
bleach
Out Pondered the Hare

In memory of Kathryn Levon

Clover

Woke up with the sweat
that doesn't make me squirm
   Not anymore.
From that dream of translucent
cobras curled round
black widow spiders blue
audible contractions as it
squeezed
   and I know full well cobras do
not constrict
   but there it was.

Skunk Anansie Charlie Big Potato
low through Sony speakers

laid horizontal on the floor
those vibrations may contribute
to the hallucinatory dream states
    at 2:42 am.
Severed heads collected and
stored in freezers like that serial
killer
or that serial killer
from a Netflix docu-series

It doesn't set a good example for
the children,
    she told me,
sleeping in the basement.
She has stopped telling me so
often
    Lately
Reminds me to take my pills at
breakfast
the other before bed.

There was a boy in a bucket
    I poured lukewarm water over
his head with a Styrofoam cup
He looked up at me
then down.

Asked me what I do for work
Told him a mid-level marketing
manager
for a mid-size company in the
Midwest.
Gave him a pat on the head.
    'Don't pat the head of an
astronaut.' 'How old are you?'
'Seven.'

My daughter dropped her spoon
Clanked on the floor
she started crying.

Astronaut gone
She ate Lucky Charms
New spoon.
Kissed her head
    told her accidents happen.

It's not healthy, she told me,
    to feed our children
sugary cereal.
We shouldn't feed sugary cereal
to our *child*, I responded.
    She slapped me,

told me to fuck off with my
syntax.

A bird flew into the window
Lucy went to it
watched it die.
I told her the bird was fine.

It's not good, my wife told me, to
lie to the children.

Child.

Lucy colored a cardboard box
    Birds and nests and seeds
I told her how pretty it was.
She asked if Birdie would like it
Of course.
Filled the box
with branches plum with
pinecones

I've run knives
through a large piece of plywood.
Cut handles
Secured them with masking tape

When it's time I will place it on
the trampoline
    climb out our bedroom
window
    dive backwards from the roof
and see whose side God is on.

    When the time is right.

My responsibility
to dig a grave for Birdie
Told them after work
They countered 'now'
I countered 'lunch'
I'll be late today

The flower garden
My wife
Lucy, box
Me, a spade

The boy in the bucket
watched me dig.
    'Call me Danny.' 'I'm not going
to call you Danny.' 'I know about
the trampoline, do they?'

Elasticity will keep me safe
Cutting shallow into the flesh.

'90 miles an hour down I-55 and
a jerk of the steering wheel into a
guardrail halfway to New Orleans
is the way to do it.'
    Danny had thought this
through

Work
Dead bird residuals on the
steering wheel
Parked nearest the exit
Don't trust those people
with "VP" or "C" in titles.

The vampire girls in graphic
design
keep the lights off
Southeast end for marketing
Southwest sales
    High wall cubicles
We are not brave to battle
vampires

The company has found room
in the budget for desk lamps

Redhead dyed office
administrator gives ballpoint pens
company name
company logo
Shows her cleavage
    Make the men ravenous
    Make the women jealous
    She's got age, going to turn

Man who calls himself boss
converted an office to a 'thinking'
room.
Flowy flowery art walls
    Keurig
    Mini fridge
Sales and finance actively
undermining effort.
    My manager walked behind my
cubicle
    kicked my chair
    Grunted
    then left for Canada.

30-minute lunch

A goose nesting by bushes
Sub sandwich
in random office parking lot
Returned
Watched the CEO smash the
eggs
chase the goose.
'I would have broken its neck if I
could've caught it'
Laughed,
then got into his Porsche.

Circle Back

On Teams
Zoom
morning coffee agenda
　you got gorgeous Dell
monitors
fluttered spreadsheets
Circle back Tuesday
　get back to me when you see
the sun
　　the power, he whispered
stays in the emails
you're not cc'd on
　off-brand unauthorized
Teams calls in late hour owl hoots
infused whiskey on breath
men who dress with a belt

    business socks
stand out slightly with
    curated patterns, muted
palettes
doesn't matter how short her skirt
gets
still a day older
in the VP's heart
    ordered – no – ordained in
Salesforce self-worth
coiled around analytics
    numbers green, numbers red
Show him the desk
Make him proud in hitched skirts
for just one more day
    This Day
Make it to that invisible irrational
insignificant number
    Then you'll tell him nothing
You won't have to
And they'll put you in there, put a
VP in front of your title
So everyone knows
    What a truly valid
    Truly meaningful life
    You have lived.

An Emu
Resting

Ego wrestling.
An emu resting.
A moral compass with variables.
Definitive definitions of
psychopathy that ignores
sociological implications.
Social imperfections.

If you're not contemplating
suicide
every three days you aren't living.

Saw a Mercedes SUV
with several 26.2 bumper stickers.

Saw them at the stoplight and
fuck
I wanted to murder them.
They needed it. They deserved it.
It would have been the right
thing to do.

Couches
70s relics
cut into the apartment corner.
Target clearance lamp sat on
garbage night driveway find end
table.
Mustard-yellow where the color
stayed
Standard-issued beige nothing
where worn.
The second forest green shag
if you perceive nature in putrid
green.

Three days since she put a brick
through my car window.
Two days since we said we
couldn't live without each other.
She just left. Suggested she would
return at her designated lunch

hour from administratively
assisting in an office park behind
the gas station and Chipotle.

I like the way
she quietly consults
with the cat
pertaining to my state of mind.
I like that she wears those short
shorts
ponders where her phone
disappears based on the weather.

She finds my hidden notebooks
reads them on the toilet
the door locked.

Sometimes
for a day
or an hour

Sometimes she stays
for a day
an hour

Three months

since I've halted social media
progress.
A death date for digital
breadcrumbs.

Was a Sunday
Getting used to typewriter
keyboards and limitations of
landline.

Sadness at Google.
Confusion in the Starbucks
Rewards department.

The sin of complacency and true
adherence to compliance gives
solace to the decaying days.

I imagine myself a Mexican
migrant plucking tomatoes at
sunrise.

No, I imagine myself a corporate
tycoon entrenched in greed and
passing on those traits to a son

who's accepted a lacrosse
scholarship to Yale.

A marble mausoleum
Centered
Amid lesser mausoleums.

I imagine I'm someone of
importance, resources, and
worthy of remembering on the
CNN chyron.

You American Patriot

Tick.
Tock, you American patriot.
Texas Gun Laws got me strapped
Ain't no papers to cross state
lines
Got no checkpoints for AR-15
rounds
Seatbelt and five over
Hands off the GPS
You law-abiding American citizen
Smirking in the wind thinking
How the bullets click into place
You Goddamn American Patriot

A Racoon Climbing on a Roof with Clay Shingles

A man called Sigmund
They called him Sigmund
Let his wet fingertips run infinite
lengths
Around clay
Pushed the pedal
Imagined himself a metal
drummer
Kicking bass
Inside the wooden shack

At property rear
Where horses neighed
Imagined freedom from fence
A chill from that first Autumnal
apparition
Check God's breath with stocked
firewood
He pushed the pedal and clay
went
With wet fingertips
For new figurines on birch
benches
A ballerina
A horse
A steamer ship
A cat reposed

A Middle-Age Housewife with Caustic Gore Wine

She put sand inside her bathing
suit
To feel something more when she
returned home

Drove with her right hand
grasping her left wrist over
bridges
So she didn't let the covert
thoughts manifest into action

Left her lighter in the center
console
So she didn't set flame to the
cheerful saleswoman at the
makeup counter
Where the plethora perfumes
mutate and coalesce into madness
Unrestrained by purse strings on
the eastern wall
Perfect halved mannequin legs
snug in yoga pants over western
shoulders
Under pop music bubblegum
apple pie thousand watt halogens

Found exodus and borrowed a
lighter from a girl half her age
near the dumpsters
The girl thought to herself I hope
I never turn out like her
The woman thought to herself
There will be the same bridges on
the return

Under Orange Lamps Near Pink Shutters

Said 13 on the radio dial
Sent her scrambling
For the AC
Didn't wake the Texas boy
brought north in the passenger
seat
Cracked the window for dead
desert air
Found Jesus on 94.1
and left him there until the devil
Caught in her throat
Tempted her to pull over

Exit 107
The Amigo Inn pink shutters
tinted orange
From parking lot lamps over glass
shard pavement
Where pieces were pushed into a
pile by a mustachioed man
who disappeared
And in his place una mujer
clutched to shopping cart
cleaning supplies and there she
gasped
Where Mary herself had
presented in the night previous
broken
Under orange lamps near pink
shutters

A Good Day it Was

Spent the week on sedatives
  Doused. Dosed, redeemed.
Feel strange
  in the company of elderly men
insisting
on pushing themselves up
from grocery store scooters to
  prove
they have what it takes
to slide their debit card into the
machine.
Dosed in lines
Doused in pastel dresses to
remind myself

how it feels
        in the darkness—free to
become whatever
that elderly man grunted.
Persisted.
    Joked to the cashier clerk a
minor
Of age. Gaps. How it goes.
    Took several moments to
describe that Honda motorcycle
he once owned.
Ten cases of Coca-Cola and six
bottles of Gatorade
    That'll get him home
Fall into the recliner
    And mutter how good a day it
was
and a good day it was.

Living Loosely Under a Pandemic Blue Sky

Drinking from the sink
in a darkened bathroom
Toes enmeshed in the rug
A woolen sock and a pair
of pajama bottoms
Living loosely under a pandemic
blue sky
Living with the blue sleeping pills
that have gone adverse
And I wake at 2 in the morning

to recount dreams of ex-lovers
and a woman
I don't know
with her breasts exposed so I
open
a door to let the dog outside
and drive my car through a
parking garage with no exits until
I realize
that there is work to be done
tomorrow
and I should give sleep focus
I'm drinking from the sink
in a darkened bathroom
the fridge hums
someone is snoring

That Obese Kind of Mid-40s

Ants.
Two weeks in L.A.
New home smells of cat vomit
and urine.
Four days driving for this
    I remind myself.
New roommate
That obese kind of mid-40s
    cancer survivor
    obese
    just found God.
The smell.
Permeates nostrils the lingering
and you cannot lose it.

Spent four days on knees
scrubbing brown tile eggshell
white.
Spent four days building my
triceps with a vacuum
and his bedroom remains.
That obese kind of mid-40s
    Spiderman obsessive
on bumpers
on t-shirts
on shelfs action-figured.
His bedroom remains.
Oversized white underwear
strewn about comic book boxes,
weeks old cat food reeking and
rotting in Gladware containers.
    His cat has defected to my
bedroom.
Ants. They crawled unison
through the window screen
    Through cracks in the drywall
near the sill
    Hidden in the closet and ran
upon my slow-leaking air
mattress.
Hundreds. Thousands.

I took to them with paper towel
anger and smashed.
Vacuumed them into canisters
    And felt their sad cylindrical
confusion
    as I fell asleep and woke at 4
A.M. on the floor.

A Box I Choose

Placed wooden pallets
on concrete pads
in back warehouses
they found him in the shower
Drink and smoke got him
when he added the pills
    they go down so easy
Spread his ashes on the football
field
    Gutted, absolutely
        Gutted
Drove one thousand thirty two
miles
for an Asian girl's embrace only
to return

to honey lacquered mediocrity
sweating in a basement apartment
Felt like Fall leaves composting in
gutters
    Along curbs that snake through
cavernous exurban roads
Felt like rejection ruminating in
holes
On pickup truck bed memories
Warm lager pulled from broken
garage refrigerators
I'm chasing him down
    Got the drink
    Got the smoke
So easy

Apathetic Mack

All the boy wanted
when he dunked his head
into the toilet
was to know, really know,
that the police were no longer
lingering
in the living room
maybe, just maybe, if he kept his
head down
long enough
they would just go away,

Hushed tones
one of these boys
they might have a litigious father

By the book, sergeant
Frisked the boy, ain't nothing
going down the toilet.

Sopped head wet hairs blond
Drip
Sit down, son.

Drip

Folding chair
Coffee table drug den
paraphernalia
Five boys eyes dilated
Narc #122
Opened the blinds—the signal
Brought K9
Get these boys, by the book.

The boy dripped
Bounced his leg

Eyes dilated, bouncing leg,
nervousness
He's the one we want.

Trying Hard to Smell Decent

Wet nap fingers
Pork ribs get lost in the bones
Sucks the fingers and gulps down
pink lemonade crushed ice

Smooth jazz speaker covers
spackled with dried sauce
He bends over the register
Click clack two-inch paper rolls
And it rolls and he bends over the
register
Coughs into the crook of his
elbow

Plastic silverware
Hard plastic trays
Turns off the lights
Three hard presses against the
dispenser
with coarse skin
wrinkled from water water water
and aching joints
Slime pink soap trying hard to
smell decent
Runs the water
And every time he hears the train
whistle behind the alley
He wonders where it all went

A Man You Can Trust

Picked up on the Social
and it made him a believer
Chinese AI on blast
Got him lusting on knees at
Putin's feet
Got him out of that mud fuck
liberal logic

Picked up on the Teleprompter
lurched in Christ tattooed on one
shin
an orange baboon the other
and it made him a believer

Algorithms squeezed until
constricted throats gurgled

Picked up on the Podcast
Abstracts read of pseudo-science
publications by shaved head
pontificators
engorged on citations
that cite shit
made him a believer
and got himself a bumper sticker
to fornicate with the others

Picked up on the Emails that
inundate
bubbled with rage and in that rage
clicked donate
to what? he didn't care to read the
fine print
he's got the faith and details make
his brain go mud fuck
    and we cannot have that

Picked up on the Comments
Rained down on the brown
people

waist-deep in the river through
barbed wire with their five-year
old terrorist
three-year old complicit
look south, you patriots
there's nothing north but white
heroes
with AR-15s at bowling alleys
bars
the schools (not 'our')
fuck them they got the false flags
she told him
white heroes in Charlottesville
Parkland
Highland Park
Oxford
made him a believer
beleaguered
left behind
overlooked
taken over by the browns
run by the Jews
and if only, he pontificated, if
only the blacks and finally
there's a man
a man he could trust

and put those true traitors where
they belong
so sayeth the social
teleprompters
podcasts
in emails and they thunder in
ALL CAPS through comment
feeds

Where They Lay Mama

That's where Mama
got the coma
bent down to the tulips
where Pa found her
pressed against the oak
picked her up and slung her
over his shoulder

That's where Mama
looked like she was flying
at once took on the bark
from where pressed

The porch

where they lay Mama
And that Preacher come
And that Man in the suit
Brought his Cadillac
Pulled up and all the boys
Took to peeking the interior

Where the Women
in flower dresses and felt
Feathers that shot out
from hatted heads
Ginger curls
Straight bourbon blonde
Chestnut in bows
on the Women in flower dresses
that sat
with appointed handkerchiefs
to take the pain from Mama
cause she got the coma
and Pa found her

A Needle Tip

Wiped and sanded flattened
Pulled through strands of yarn
A needle tip
Sky Daddy's got me and I'm
going
To the infinity of time
To live a million years from my
children
And still able to whisper in their
ears
A flashed molecule dancing on
Senturius 17B
As we watch Saturday Morning
Cartoons
Sky Daddy I'm good for the debt
Wink

Seen her dance ballet nine
minutes ago
Hugged her
Handed bouquet
Hoped she'll still be dancing
When there's gray in my beard
and eight minutes ago slung
through perpetual
memories that embarrass me and
Sky Daddy
is telling me that no one
remembers those things
And I taught my son to ride his
bicycle
while ants consumed the moon
Tuesday is Wednesday
and also last Monday
pulled through strands of yarn
Tomorrow
Sky Daddy explains
Will taste like unripe strawberries
Flow like the vines on Sunday's
barn walls
Exude the loudest quiet you will
ever know
Where the Saturday Morning
Cartoons collapse

on the ballet stage in a flash of
molecular chaos
so serene
Yes, Sky Daddy,
so serene

bleach

Lacquered walls
in white slathered bleach
masked the olfactory
heroin withdrawals amid needles
arranged in heart shape
drip drip that salty blood
Splashed the diluted onto eggshell
white ceilings and let it rain down
and drip drip
soaked a Chase Bank rain poncho
giveaway procured in email
address cash

Opened a window so the natural
stench of human habitation in the

alley could suck down the fumes
and choke
And choke

Scraped the walls through EPA
approved paint to get to lead
layers
She floundered on a mattress on
some mental crack induced by a
masked man
donned in polyester brown
'I'd rather be fishing'
embroidered on a fat tie above a
trout and he took off his belt
beat her good
like that scamp boy when he stole
his sister's ice cream cone
let that wry smile smack across
his face
and pushed that cone into the dirt
beat her good
like that little shit
Her loan will outlive her
so suit and tie let fly on her bare
ass
and dropped her here
headed for his next appointment

tucked in deep away from the
baristas
with black coffee two sugars
with his black binder
his black contracts
'I've got words' and he spoke

Pulled hard at the cream carpet
cut it around the pink flamingo
sofa
Sat himself down two hours ago
iPhone on full bars
twenty percent batteries
Closing the deal on an internet
slut who's found fame peeing into
custom coffee mugs where men
can have their name and face
imprinted on the side while she
empties herself

She is on her way
Told him she can't urinate in here

Splattered the lead layers with
new bleach
Higher concentration
Closed the windows

Deep breaths to make it quicker if
it wants to come
'I'm not dead,' she whispered
from the mattress
'Do you want to be dead?'
'No.'

Opened the windows
Diluted mixture
Dropped the yellow sponge and
promised not to look in any
mirrors until the burnt flesh scent
diminishes
Rearranged the needles
Made an arrow that pointed to
the pink flamingo couch
Walked to the couch
'I'm not dead.'
Five percent batteries

Let her in
in ecru trench coat
A cheap perfume mist
that made the bleach brilliant
Reached in her coat and thrust a
white coffee mug towards the
pink flamingo

Mondays, am I Right?
Chugged water from a translucent
blue Nalgene bottle

Put his iPhone in his pocket
Wrote his name in black Sharpie
above *Mondays*
Watched her shed down to red
panties pulled them aside
Realized she's the cleanest that's
been in this apartment
Asked her to be a roommate
She handed the mug to him
Four percent batteries
Dressed she left

A higher mixture
Scrubbed the ceiling
Thick bristles that flaked the paint
Covered the mattress
The girl
who was floundering and singing
softly some country love song
I'm going to lay with her
after the bleach
and ask her to sing it to me

Bubbly Soft

I'm waiting for
forecasted dreams
that bubble softly
percolate in the mixture
.15mg Ativan
30mg Paxil
3oz Buffalo Trace
1g Bubble Gum Pop sativa 29.72
THC
1 Unisom Sleep Tab

They come
dreams bubbly soft
Percolating
Vivid
Wild

Excruciatingly perfect
Until she punches me in the arm
Shakes me by my ear
to tell me I haven't taken a breath
In twenty seconds and she shows
me the timer
on her phone so I deny
as I was there in the vivid and
wild
excruciatingly perfect

Trucker

The trucker was thorough, and
when he noticed
the latch open atop the milk
tanker
and the other man had gone
he climbed the ladder
and walked the flattened steel
to close the latch.

As he turned his foot slid
fell to the gravel
his back struck
his head.

Another man came
ambulance

an hour to the hospital bleeding
out fractured skull
bruising on arms
legs
no pain meds for six hours
maybe more
wait for the blood thinners to
wear off.

His wife came
held his trembling hand
he had lost the bass in his voice
his eyes explored as nothing else
could save the pain.

She slept in a chair besides him
and in the morning they took his
pain away
set his bones.
His phone vibrated and she
answered
Work
Asked if he had received the
flowers and told her
to tell him
that he was fired

no longer able to perform duties
as required.

She told him
and he laughed
asked her if they could get a kitten
an orange one
and he *booped* an imaginary kitten
nose.

Union Pacific Northwest

Based and hopeless on Metra
express trains towards Chicago
Union Pacific Northwest
Des Plaines raised
a potent man
vigor-grind-vigor
dropped his bag and flipped the
seat
Bopped his head on renegade jazz
Irving Park got the girl
intense YouTube rabbit hole
flunked out of med school no she
left she'll tell you
Not for her

The Evanston hierarchy and
spent her evenings
in a boxing gym above a dry
cleaners
Rolls herself in foam for clicks
Clamps her nipples for
subscriptions
Clybourn Casio musician played
us out slow into OTC
Spoke stories into an almost
empty Coca-Cola plastic bottle
His spit mixed in fake caramel
colorization
King of Fiji reincarnated and
none of this matters
None of this
Really matters
And that is why
He needs your attention
In your button down polos
Plaid skirts and leather shoes and
messenger bags
Caramel lattes and quick breakfast
options for those who grind and
are making it
known on LinkedIn
below powerfully posed portraits

Eyes stuck in the pixels and ears consumed by Airpods always listening for the next business opportunity.

Rubbing the Tar Black Beauty of Man's Triumph

Overgrown in sewage sin sparked
in the oils that ran the length of
the culvert

Where the reeds wilt in rust
discolored veins and herons wade
through sludge to adhere to
migratory patterns listed in
birding magazines and the
authoritative editions

Plucking slick plumes off
decaying heron carcasses

Rubbing the tar black beauty of
man's triumph
Smearing it with oil-stained
fingers burnt of prints
from those evasion years
War paint on my forehead and
down cheeks

Waiting prone in the sticky sin
goo
head raised in wait
Fingernails dug into dirt flung a
bag of nails across the pavement
and waited for the pop pop pop
crash splash

And you can smell your prey
from the distance
Frightened mother baby in back
seat
Father masochist strapped for
road rage

The aroma of a teenage waitress'
apron in the backseat of a Toyota
Camry
cake layered in grease ketchup
whipped cream

If you see my face on the news
feeds
know that I tried my best
to be someone else
when they pump my lungs full of
Alabama nitrogen

route 72 down to the culvert
the one I've shown you before
you knew *me*
scrub those herons with Dawn
liquid dish soap
and take some of the oil-stained
sin from this world

Algorithmic Calm in a Pretty Bowed IPO Box

I'm going to have to look after
you
They put a guitar in your hands
said smile
flashbulbs and ring lights
that's great
spiked your hair wardrobe change
punk rock golfer confuse the
algorithm
make it drip
ooze with tangential data
Combed it down

dressed you in a suit next to a
Black man in a suit next to an
Indian in a suit and they had a
spreadsheet that checked
everything the AI needed

Monkey equals Black man
Tweak it
Monkey does not equal Black
man
Good. Good. Shit.
White man in suit disappeared.
Too far. Tweak it
Steal only enough
Find that loophole law that fucks
those pretentious artists
They got the claims
We got the lawyers
Endless litigation pouring out of
yachts parked inside yachts built
from burned out Uber drivers and
their unattainable automobile
repairs from DoorDash peons
who snapped at Taco Bell
workers when they should have
been in the offices fingering tech
bros with Bowie knives and

expanding those cavities with
rounds

10 million books published in
2026 written by [AI] John Peters
from Columbus Ohio [thriller, in
the style of Dan Brown] and [AI]
Sally Mayforth, grandmother,
flower tender, from San Bruno
California [gardening, in the style
of all gardening books we've
scraped]

Last Night on the Forest Floor

I. The Forest

Dark
I woke
Shadowy blur as my eyes adjusted

A moment,
length of time to clarify my eyes
Buddy Holly frames Retro-
looking spectacles
that poked her cheek when I'd
go in for a kiss.

Sitting against a tree.

Dried leaves crunch under body

Pocket phone vibrations
    Reminder
    Shrink Appt.
    Dr. Vassar
    9:30

Recent calls.
Jessica
Mike
Ben
Jessica
Jake
Patrick
Mike
Jessica

Call me, I would implore
Spoken words sing
Three in the morning
Clouds obscured moon moved
eastward
Waxing gibbous
Bright
Tree limbs bare
    mostly

3 A.M.
Made small swirls of leaves
my backpack got two pens

A mechanical pencil.
Gum wrappers
Bound book of M.C. Escher
paintings.
Half-full plastic bottle raspberry
flavored iced tea. French/English
Index cards Two spiral
notebooks.
Blue Bic lighter.

A breeze sauntered
rustled remaining leaves clinging
to branches
Had to get warm
Firewood
Dead leaves
Orange glow crackle split

II. The Playground

Morning
I woke
Two squirrels

Sat up
wiped the dirt
A car beyond the forest
Loud, far
Legs sore as I stood
No vibrations
No signal
walked for civilization
A signpost subtle indication

Found a beaten path
Cars
Pickup trucks
Perhaps
Engines loud
Morning warmed
Sparrows
Cardinals
Aware of me, disinterested

Pocket phone vibrations
  Reminder
  Shrink Appt.
  Dr. Vassar
  9:30

Voices

Children's voices
Laughter, delight

Path bent
Clearing
Playground everything steel

Slide
Monkey bars
Little horses red
blue on springs

Mothers wore flower print
dresses
Faux leather coats
sat on wooden benches at the
edges
Spoke a whispered hush above
the din
Yelled out to children
Approval
Disappointment
A little boy hung upside down
from monkey bars.
Girl swung

Old cars

1970s
or 80s

Stay hidden
Follow path
No threat
Stay young
Short
Unassuming
Like you belong there

III. The Road

"Hello there, son," the man yelled
over the rebel engine
passenger-side wheels on road's
shoulder
endless prairie beyond

"Good morning, sir"
He hesitated.
"Haven't seen you around here,
you got family here?"
Blue pinstripe suit
brown fedora

Long beige trench flung over
passenger seat

"No sir."
"Well, where you headed?"
Car pointed east
"To town."
"Well, son, that's a little vague as
there are two towns you could
reasonably walk to."
"The one that is this way,"
I pointed west.
"Ah, Pointsville," he said
sympathetically. "Probably got an
hour, maybe two, ahead of you
on foot."
"Is, uh, the other town closer?"
"It could be."
"Which town should I go to?"
"Well, I wouldn't know that,
would I?"
"What's the other town's name?"
"Belle Fountaine."
Rubbed dirt with my shoe "That's
actually where I'm heading. I
must've got turned around."
He stared at me

an awkward moment
then ahead down the road.
"I can give you a ride, son."

IV. The Cadillac

Small metal case on dashboard
Handed me a business card. "My
name's Roy. Roy Carter. I sell life
insurance."
"Samuel," I paused. "Morelle."
Car growled in gear
drove down the road.

"You any good?"
"At what?"
"At selling life insurance."
"Son, I'm the best damn life
insurance agent in the entire state.
Got a plaque at home on the
mantel and everything."
"Why not keep it in your office?"
"I'm never in my office, I'm
either at home or on the road.
The road is where the people are.
The road," he paused for effect,

"is where life is, where life
happens."

V. The Diner

Never liked eggs
Runny snot texture
or yellow brained scrambled.
Roy suggested over-medium
Ate them all
Hash browns
Bacon
Orange Juice

Waitress smiled
I blushed teenage uncertainty
Her light brown hair
attached with bobby pins
under a paper white hat

"Thank you for breakfast."
"It was my pleasure, son."

Pocket phone vibrations
  Reminder
  Shrink Appt.
  Dr. Vassar

Now

Recent calls.
Jessica
Jessica
Mike
Ben
Jessica
Jake
Patrick
Mike
Jessica

Outside the Belle Fountaine
Diner
Steadied on the hood of a 1970s
Ford Fiesta
Fought it
Lost
Vomited the eggs
hash browns
the bacon on to the pavement
between the Fiesta
and a Chevy Impala
Thick saliva dripped down my
chin
onto my shirt

Spun
Fought it
Slid to the ground

They gathered
Men in suits
Women, children pressed against
legs
The waitress
  Graceful
  Loving
Brushed my hair with her fingers
I woke
Shadowy blur as my eyes adjusted
White hat simulated nurse
tended to smallpox
measles
polio
iron lungs
Smiled I smiled
told the Black cook
soiled apron
black frayed hairnet
it's okay
he opened the door
bell hung by string
and disappeared into the diner

Sat up
as did she
Her eyes
Lily soft pale with freckles
Cleavage made it move
Infatuation lust love
bungled in teenage boy synapses

Pocket phone vibrations
　Reminder
　Shrink Appt.
　Dr. Vassar
　Overdue

Recent calls.
Jessica
Jessica
Jessica
Mike
Ben
Jessica
Jake
Patrick
Mike
Jessica

Wherein Wonderland

Wherein Wonderland flowed
acid-laced waterfalls
Flesh blessed, soaked in mercury
exfoliation drops rubbed into skin
Eyelash radium girls green glow
Skipping through bramble and
wild grass
Feathered whiskers red whispered
on felines
Hopping over turtles painted
sepia
Lined on lily pads float and a
buoyant bob
Silicone seeping tree sap

Flowed down to acid-laced
waterfalls
Where does she go from here?

5:13 on a Wednesday

Pulled *The Soft Machine* off the
shelf
Homosexual cross-border
escapades pile on
as I drink a grande mocha and
wonder
what that old couple are thinking
as they stare
probably not corkscrewing a
foreign boy in Mexico
Fuck
What if that is *exactly* what they
are thinking about?

Those dirty, dirty white suburban
Americans at Starbucks
in Long Grove, Illinois
at 4:37 on a Wednesday
I love them.

Pulled *Love is a Dog From Hell*
from the shelf
Dirty smut apartments
humid sweat skin where the
cigarette smoke pools
Conquests compile as Bukowski
finds faults in their breasts and
wrinkles and pronunciations of
the word 'narrow'
'snatch'
'fleeting'
'man-whore'

Watched the financial consultant
pull acid-free glossy papers from
his portfolio
Handed it to the woman
while she occupied
her child with milk and a sugar-
free cookie

And while she studied the charts -
pies and lines and columns of red
purple blue within brand
standards
He drifted off into past conquests
Their names-could he remember
The smell of the room
The smell of *her*
The city
Her number and where she fit in
the sequence of girls who took
their clothes off for him
And between poems I glanced at
him
Sipped a cinnamon dolce latte
knew his thoughts
and his fingers flit under the table
as he counted off the girls
That proud conquistador
at Starbucks
in Long Grove, Illinois
at 5:13 on a Wednesday

Sober

Wake
Coffee and a cigarette
Local news
The pretty weather girl
Whom you imagine wants you
Based solely on proximity
Power button
Password
Emails
Teams
Imagined emergencies
that warrant
6am alerts
Conference calls
Agendas and action items and
next steps

Frozen pasta and strawberry
banana yogurt
Coffee and a cigarette
5pm east coast—good enough
Evening news
Marla's on maternity leave
Bill's on weather
Gym
The pretty yoga pants girl
Whom you imagine wants you
Based solely on proximity

A Savior

He left home
followed the tracks
somehow heard of salvation
a savior
Filled his pockets with small
secrets
Dug his hands to keep them
hidden

Had faith along the path
Side-eyed the doubters behind
tinted train car windows
traveling the swath

Took the keep-going pills
Put his faith atop the track

and let the wheels test

Cracked a memory with a twitch
Grandad sunlit in the pews
as each parishioner passed
with a solemn nod
and he, reclined, suspenders
bursting across his broad body
returned each
with an almost imperceptible tick
in the corners
where his lips met

And here he was
Home beyond the horizon
Following an assumed salvation
A savior
In the August heat
Along the tracks and the crickets
and the strangeness
of dry brush bristling his calves

Through Soft Skin

Marks left
Scars
Where nails dug deep
Where glass shards slit
through soft skin
She wants to move like a bird
Flow like wild love in forests
Where there are no marks
No scars

Hoon

Rose between sunflowers
in fields
Rows of mud standing tall
after summer showers
Rouse from slumber
in dreams indescribable
Rue on river banks
where the sun feeds
One of these days this will die,
Shannon
and so will me,
and so will you

My Dear,
Ignore the War

My dear
Ignore the war
Go to town
Wait near the bar
for a young man
Red roosters stitched to his
cuffed collared eggshell white
And when he orders you a white
rose cosmopolitan
you'll know he's me
Take softly his coarse hand
Hardened days wrenching pipe
Pull him to the wooden floor
Nearest the band

The standup bass
Let him lead
and when you feel it
you'll know he's me

My baby
Forget the war
Take him out the back door
Pull his strings
Slip past the vomitous men
hunched over
who once had the world
balanced and broken to their will
Go left into the alley
moist with lust
Pull up your summer knit dress
Lead him in
and when you feel it
you'll know he's me

Set About the Whores

Maybe misplaced faith
Set about the whores
Contemplated offers
Leather around ankles
Chanel and shame aroma
Slept hard
Woke with wallet empty
Whore above me
insisting on pancakes with
blueberry syrup

He's Just Got To

Think I'll step out for a moment
for clear visuals
to clear the corruption from my
breaths
see nature as a secondary
hierarchy—not mental
antagonism
to believe in the future—no
cycles
or repetitious relationships
for a smoke
Walk once
24-hour Coney Island facades at
overrun office buildings

conformity beckons
reconciliation with the youth
Who? Him?
He's got the responsibility of pure
superiority
He's got to complete tattered
sentences
with a mouth full of chili cheese
French fries
He's just got to.

March 11, 2000

Two Erins from Ohio
Cherry blonds like tongues
enmeshed under summer rain
enjoined in young skin
Feels like we've the makings
of some radical movement
Ignore the whispers
Do not become a casualty of
conformity
Not tonight

Downstairs two boys are
drowned in alcohol
feasting their eyes on an obese
girl touching herself
swaying to seduce

with a tear tracing down her
cheek

The Erins promised me
a lesbian show
and fell asleep in a tangle of low
cut shirts and silver necklaces
I'm having a smoke
Reading the scrap paper phone
number
And wondering
Which Erin will answer
When I call 734-487-xxxx

Shedding Clothes and Bruising Skin

Just a little more
to make me perfect
or, maybe, whole.
This place hidden in
bullet-proof vaults that hinder
God's existence.
The remaining children
  the city children
not immune to diversion
true ideals borne of ketamine
and limitless drama.

To put ourselves in holes is
fallacy—we know not where the
holes lay
    Yet we fall.

Belief in heroics,
of what *I* would do
inundated in that peril.
Put in place common mind
that produces normality
in a steady current.
Find peace
with *her*
Speak of love
with *her*
Of fear and death
And let it go
Shedding clothes and bruising
skin.

My Native Girl

Children lost on a school bus
dead in town square
my Native girl
her cancer, her hair.

White Sat

White had made it
responded to emails in timely
fashion
accepted letters with vigor
was proud, so proud
of his associate level
the brass sign pinned to cubicle
business cards with *his name*

He told Pink
and Pink said 'I'm beautiful.'
'Feeling great' White responded,
chuckled.

White sat late
under fluorescents

read letters
really read them
felt them.

White sat early
liked how the sun would ricochet
between buildings and warm
windows.

White hummed
typed
Hummed like grandfather
who played trumpet
Typed and imagined if touching
his lips to the brass
was the same

White printed and signed each
letter blue
so they'd know
licked pre-addressed envelopes
and when it was time,
went to Green.

'I'm going to Los Angeles,' Green
told him
She had for years.

Green puts stamps on envelopes. That is
what she does.
He told his reflection
in pressed pajamas.
That, is why she is here.

Yellow visited at 11.
Every day.
'How's White today?'
'Fine.'
'Good.'

Yellow never found his office,
never wore a tie
'How's White today?'
'The letters?'
'Good.'

No more letters
White went to Pink
'The letters?'
'I'm beautiful'

White hummed
Crimson walked briskly
went to Green

her mascara smeared and wet
'Looks like a racoon'
White muttered and Green heard.

In pressed pajamas
White wondered about Pink
worried about Green
Hummed, thumbed through
stacks of business cards
his name
'Associate'
White had made it.

Politic
Erstwhile

Politic erstwhile
threatened I threaten
Push down hard
on suit donned con men
Shame hath
no place
in hallowed halls
consecrated by the inherited
ideals of fuckboys high on
erection pills
and country cunts lusting for
whore level attention
who power piss faux idealism
reviewed and ascertained

as sin from on high
nowhere in their sermons
when they reclaim their time
is a whisper
of the poor
the sick
the hungry

A Wheezing Cough

He was ready
inhaled
geared for a wheezing cough
as they would pass him
they did pass him
what a horrible wretched man
he thought they thought
he thought fuck you, you stupid
bitches
he thought they would pass him
geared himself up
and they did pass him
through automated sliding doors
into the mall

She Attracts Glitter

Yells after every evening shower
she attracts glitter
it settles deep into skin
I'll think of you next year

Hey, This is Techno

High school girls in short skirts
had got themselves positioned
with shirtless new boys in white
visors and handled glow sticks

and were always polite to the old
man stilt man straw hat been
tripping since 1973

14 year old boys crowd surfed
while 22 year old boys whispered
'hey man, this is techno'

Paramedics grunted and followed
their ears for the unconscious,
scavenged the Hart Plaza
concrete
vultures for overdoses.

Pantene representatives made
their $14/hour handing out
sample sizes of shampoo and
conditioner. A kid in line for
strong roots and manageable hair
asked another kid looking to up
his style, 'hey man, how was jail?'

A homeless man sat on the
bench. Had this scraggly beard
and the curls went everywhere.
Another man joined him, set
down his own garbage bag and
duffle.

I cut through the mob of rich
white kids from money rains on
the suburbs who know the cops
won't let them die tonight and
handed the men my Pantene.

Harmonica

It's a beautiful fall morning.
I tried to do the dishes,
but the sink is clogged.
I got my harmonica.

Are you ready for a cookieless world?

Are your webinars stuck in the past? I remember her getting up, screaming. Shaking, unable to sleep.

Cultivate a PMM Capability to Optimize Your GTM. I can help you. I love you. Let's get a call on the calendar. A placeholder. For my love (that's you).

Are you getting the most out of your Field Marketing program? Stripped down, covered in wet sand like glitter. Raise your ROI.

Come on, I'll show you a good
time down by the docks.

Marketing Orchestration, B2B
Customer Experience, Marketing
Workflows, and More! Ask me
how and I'll reveal everything that
glistens.

Are you ready for a cookieless
world? He found the pistol
loaded in the gravel pits, said
goodbye, and wished one last
time a fisherman.